WHAT IT MEANS TO BE

SERIES

PUBLISHER	Joseph R. DeVarennes
PUBLICATION DIRECTOR	Kenneth H. Pearson
ADVISORS	Roger Aubin
	Robert Furlonger
PROJECT CO-ORDINATOR	Sarah Swartz
EDITORIAL MANAGER	Jocelyn Smyth
EDITORS	Ann Martin
	Shelley McGuinness
	Robin Rivers
	Mayta Tannenbaum
PRODUCTION MANAGER	Ernest Homewood
PRODUCTION ASSISTANTS	Kathy Kishimoto
	Douglas Parker
PUBLICATION ADMINISTRATOR	Clare Adam

Canadian Cataloguing in Publication Data

Dickie, Alison
  Kind

(What it means to be; v. 3)
ISBN 0-7172-2227-6

1. Kindness — Juvenile literature.
I. Title.   II. Series.

BJ1533.K5D53 1987   j158'.2   C86-095059-X

WHAT IT MEANS TO BE...

KIND

Written by
Alison Dickie

Illustrated by
Steve Pileggi

Being kind means telling friends that you like them.

Hannah and Mitchell were bouncing a big red ball back and forth. They had been throwing and catching for a long time, when Hannah began to giggle and make funny faces at Mitchell. Mitchell began to giggle too, and pretty soon they both started to laugh. They laughed so hard they couldn't throw or catch properly. This made them laugh even harder. They fell on the lawn laughing at each other.

Hannah looked at Mitchell and said between giggles, "I like you a lot because it's so easy to make you laugh."

"I like you too, Hannah, because you make me laugh and you don't make fun of me. You just laugh at silly things with me."

You can be kind just by telling people that you enjoy their company. Chances are they enjoy your company too. A kind remark makes everyone feel good.

Being kind means sharing.

Kim glided easily down the sidewalk on her new roller skates. She crunched along over the newly fallen leaves and stopped when she got to Colette's house.

"Hey Colette, come and look at my new skates. We can go to the park and play."

Colette felt jealous and didn't say anything at first. Then she said, "Those are beautiful skates, Kim. But I don't have skates. And anyway, I couldn't keep up with you."

"Never mind, Colette. Our feet are about the same size. We can take turns," said Kim. "That's more fun than skating by myself."

Sometimes when you get something new, friends won't have the same thing. You can be kind by offering to let your friends play with your new toy. Chances are they will be kind to you by letting you play with their new toys some other time.

Kindness is trying to understand other people's feelings.

It was a bright autumn day, and Jason came out of the school feeling wonderful. He had just read a story aloud to his class and couldn't wait to tell his parents. He ran around the corner, out of the playground and onto the sidewalk. As he turned the corner, he bumped into Paul and almost knocked him down. Just in time, he put his arms around Paul.

"Sorry about that," said Jason. "I guess I was in a hurry. I didn't mean to run into you."

"I don't care what you were doing. Take off and don't bug me," Paul said in an angry voice.

Jason was very surprised and was about to get angry too. But he could see that Paul was very upset. He tried to think of what to say next, but Paul just walked off down the street without looking back. Jason was puzzled. Paul was usually friendly and cheerful. Jason decided to find out what was wrong.

When Jason caught up to him, Paul still looked very upset. His lip was trembling as if he were about to cry. "What's wrong, Paul?" Jason asked. "You aren't mad at me just because I bumped into you, are you?"

"No," said Paul. "It's only that you got to read to the class today. I could tell it was easy for you. Well, I'm still having trouble reading. I've been trying very hard, but I can't seem to get better."

Jason stood there without saying anything. He was proud of how well he could read, but he felt sad for Paul. Then he had an idea.

"Maybe I could help you with your reading," he said. "We could get together after school for a few minutes every day. I'd be glad to give you extra help."

Being kind means offering to help, especially if someone is not very good at something you do well.

Build a friend's confidence when you can.

The next day Jason and Paul got together at Paul's house. Paul's parents were pleased that Jason had taken the time to help their son.

Every day Jason said things to encourage Paul. "You can do it, Paul. I know you can," he said, as Paul sounded out the words. After several weeks, Paul gradually relaxed, and his reading began to get better. Soon he was reading a whole page without making a mistake.

One day Paul said, "Jason, you've been terrific. Thanks for helping me. I wish I could do something for you."

Jason thought for a while. Then he said, "Hockey season starts soon and I don't skate very well. Maybe you could give me a few lessons. You're a great player, Paul."

"I'd be glad to help you out, Jason!" said Paul, beaming. "Anytime."

If you help a friend in one area, your friend can help you in another. Exchanging help makes everyone feel good.

Remember occasions that are important to others.

Hannah's feet almost flew down the sidewalk. She was very excited. Today was Janice's birthday and she was going to visit her. Hannah had made a beautiful card with a gray cat on the front. She knew that cats were her friend's favorite animal.

When Janice opened the door, Hannah shouted, "Surprise! Happy birthday."

Janice looked very surprised. "Oh, Hannah, how nice of you to remember! I didn't think anyone but my family would remember my birthday."

Janice opened the card and her eyes shone. "You even remembered that cats are my favorite animal. What a beautiful card you made for me, Hannah!"

Remembering a friend's birthday is a way of showing kindness. If you can't afford a card or a present, you can make one. Or just remembering to say happy birthday is a kind thing in itself.

Animals need kindness too.

Bobby, Paul and Mitchell were walking home from school. Suddenly they heard a high-pitched chirping sound and lots of rustling behind the bushes. They looked over the hedge and saw that Sammy, the cat, had trapped a young robin and was about to pounce on it.

"Go away Sammy. That's bad!" said Bobby. Sammy jumped over the fence and disappeared.

"I think it's hurt, because it can't fly away," said Paul. "We shouldn't pick it up though, because we might hurt it. We'd better get help."

Mitchell went home to tell his mom what had happened. Bobby and Paul stayed to guard the robin in case Sammy came back.

Mitchell's mother called the animal shelter. After a while, the van from the animal shelter arrived and a man got out. The man wore special gloves and carried a box. He gently lifted the robin and put it carefully into the box. It went "cheep, cheep."

"You did the right thing by calling us," he said to Mitchell, Bobby and Paul. "This robin has a broken wing. But he's strong and I think our veterinarian will be able to help mend it nicely. Then we'll let it go again."

Even though they can't speak, animals feel pain just as people do. That's why it's especially important to be kind to them.

Being kind means helping without being asked.

Ryan had gone to play at Kim's house after school. It was nearly suppertime when he got home, but neither of his parents were there yet. His big brother, Cameron, let him into the house and then went back to doing his homework.

Ryan's dad was working late, and his mom had gone to do errands after she finished work. He knew that they would both be tired. So without being asked by anyone, Ryan set the table for supper.

"There," he thought to himself, "now Mom and Dad will have a little bit less to do when they come home."

Being kind means helping out without being asked. There are always small chores around the house that can be done.

Being kind means trying to understand people who have different customs.

"Did you have a good day in school today?" Ryan's mother asked him. "How is Joey, the new boy who just moved in down the street?"

"Oh, he wasn't in school today," replied Ryan. "The teacher said it was a special holiday for him. That's weird! How come he doesn't take holidays when the rest of us do?"

Ryan's mother looked up from her desk. "There are many kinds of people in the world with different customs and holidays," she said. "But they're all people like us and we should respect the way they do things."

"Okay," said Ryan. "But I still don't understand about his holiday."

"Well, why don't you try making friends with Joey?" his mother said. "Maybe you would understand him better if you got to know him. Besides, don't you remember what it was like to move to a new place and not have any friends?"

Joey was back in class the next day. After school, Ryan ran up to him and asked Joey if he wanted to walk home with him.

Joey was very shy at first, and he didn't say much. But after they had walked to and from school several times, the two boys were able to talk to each other more easily.

One day Ryan told Joey that what he really wanted was a home computer.

"Oh," said Joey. "Why don't you come to my house tomorrow and use ours? I'll ask my mom if you can stay for dinner afterwards."

It can be very lonely for a new person. You can be kind by talking to a new person at school or in the neighborhood. Sometimes when you are kind, there are benefits for you that you weren't even expecting.

Show kindness to a friend who gets hurt.

Janice and Tammy were skipping with Hannah. Janice and Hannah were turning the rope and singing skipping songs while Tammy jumped.

"Faster, faster," cried Tammy, while she showed off her quick moves, hopping from one foot to the other. Suddenly she tripped and fell. Hannah and Janice quickly dropped the rope and went to help her up.

Tammy wasn't hurt badly, but she felt embarrassed that she had fallen. She started to sob.

Hannah said, "There, there, Tammy. Don't cry. Anyone can fall."

Janice put her arm around Tammy, and soon Tammy stopped crying.

A kind word or a hug can help make a friend feel better after a fall. If an injury looks serious, call an adult.

Younger brothers and sisters need kindness too.

"What's wrong?" asked Jason as he left the house and found Janice sitting on the back steps with a long face.

"I'm sad because I can't find Hannah or Tammy to play with. And Mom just told me she didn't have time to take me to the park today even though she promised."

"Well," said Jason, "I'm going to the park to practice my batting. Why don't you come along?"

"You're sure you wouldn't mind?" asked Janice.

"No," said Jason. "It's fun to play with you once in a while. You can bring your baseball glove."

Sometimes younger brothers and sisters get lonely when there isn't anyone to play with. You can be kind by taking the time to play with them.

Being kind means helping younger children.

It was a few days before Halloween and all the kids were getting together after school at Kim's house. They were planning to go trick-or-treating as "the ghostly gang." Kim and Colette were going to help the younger kids make their masks.

Kim had a special box of paints. Her mother had spread out a big plastic sheet so they could work without making a mess. Hannah and Janice arrived first and Kim showed them how to use the paints.

"Here Hannah," said Kim, "I'll help you cut out your mask and you can paint it by yourself."

Then it was Janice's turn to get help. Kim said, "Hold the brush at more of an angle and you'll find the color will go on more easily."

"You're right," said Janice. "That's a much better way of doing it."

Older children can help younger ones with a special project. Putting your time aside for people is a way of showing kindness.

Kim's mother came into the room where the kids were working. "Colette and Tammy can't make it today. Their mother called to say that they are sick."

"Oh, no!" said Kim. "If Colette and Tammy are sick, they won't have time to make their masks. And then we won't be able to go out together as the ghostly gang."

"What if we all stay longer and work on their masks?" asked Hannah.

"Yes," said Janice. "That way, if they feel well on Halloween, their masks will be ready."

"That's a great idea," said Kim. The three girls quickly painted masks for their friends.

The next day, Kim, Janice and Hannah went to Colette and Tammy's house with the masks. Colette and Tammy were feeling much better, and they were happy that their friends had made them masks. "You are all terrific," said Tammy.

"Yes," said Colette smiling. "Thanks so much. I hope we can all go out for Halloween tomorrow night."

Helping a sick friend is a very kind thing to do. It also feels good to make other people happy.

Remember to return a kindness.

Tammy pulled her red wagon up the street. She put one knee on the wagon and pushed with the other foot.

"I just love my new red wagon," she said quietly to herself. When she passed Mitchell's house, she invited him to play with her.

"Go and get your wagon. We can have a race," said Tammy.

"My wagon has a broken wheel. And my dad said he couldn't get the new part until Saturday."

"That's okay. We can take turns pulling each other with my wagon," said Tammy. "I haven't forgotten how you used to let me play with your wagon nearly every day before I got mine."

Part of being kind means remembering that friends have been kind to you in the past. Do them a good turn when you get a chance.

Being kind means helping your neighbors.

Bobby was playing in the big piles of autumn leaves, sending showers of them into the air. As he played, he saw Mr. Corban walking toward him, carrying a shopping bag. Mr. Corban lived just up the street from Bobby.

As Bobby watched, he saw Mr. Corban's shopping bag break, spilling apples and cans all over the sidewalk. Bobby stopped playing and went to help Mr. Corban. He picked up Mr. Corban's apples and carried them up the street to his house.

"Thank you so much, Bobby," said Mr. Corban when they came to his door. "I don't think I could have managed without you."

_____

You can be kind to a neighbor, especially to an elderly person, by offering to run errands, carry groceries or rake leaves.

If you say something unkind, you can always apologize.

One day Janice and Hannah were playing with their dolls on Hannah's front porch. Hannah's mother had just given her some new clothes for her doll. Hannah wanted Janice to see them. After they had been playing for a while, Hannah said, "Why does your doll only have one dirty old dress?"

Janice looked at her dear old doll and started to cry. "You're mean, I'm going home." Janice ran home with her doll. She was very upset.

Hannah's mother came out of the house. "I heard what happened, Hannah. I don't think that was a very nice thing to say to Janice. How would you like it if Janice had said something like that to you?"

Hannah hung her head. "I didn't mean to make her cry. I guess I'd better go and say I'm sorry."

Hannah went off to apologize to Janice.

Sometimes we hurt other people's feeling without intending to. But if you are mean to someone, it is best to apologize.

Being kind means trying to cheer up a friend.

On Halloween night, everyone was dressed in wonderful costumes. Janice and Bobby walked up ahead, when suddenly two big kids came out of nowhere. The strangers snatched Janice and Bobby's bags of Halloween candies and ran away. When the others caught up to them, Bobby and Janice were crying.

"We only have two more blocks to go, and we lost our best treats," sniffed Janice.

"It's okay," said Jason. "We'll all walk together from now on."

Kim gave Janice and Bobby a hug. "Don't worry," said Kim. "When we get back to my house, I'll give you both some of my candies."

Janice and Bobby were still a bit upset. But as they walked along, the other kids told jokes and made them smile. By the time everyone got to Kim's house, Bobby and Janice were feeling better.

Show your friends you care when something bad has happened.

"I have an idea," said Jason, as the gang trouped into Kim's house. "Why don't we pool our treats and share them equally? That will be fair for everyone."

They all agreed that was the best idea.

After everyone had settled down at Kim's house and divided the candy, Kim's father made hot chocolate for everyone. Her mother brought out the camera and took pictures of all the kids in costume. Soon everyone was laughing and talking. They all felt happy.

Here are some ways you can show kindness:
- Help other people whenever you can.
- Think of the feelings of others.
- Learn to share.
- Include other people in your plans, especially new people.
- Think about what you can do to make someone else happy.

Printed and Bound in the United States of America